Dehydrator Delights

By Noreen Thomas

Published by   Doubting Thomas Publishing Co.
12506 20th St
North
Moorhead, MN
56560

ISBN 10: 1-4348083-0-0

ISBN 13: 978-1-4348083-0-1

Third Edition

DEDICATION

I dedicate this book to my children,
Brita, Evan, and Carsten.

As you grow older, always remember
You can do anything you set your mind to.

CONTENTS

Noreen Jo Thomas has a Bachelor of Science degree in Food and Nutrition. She teaches Dehydrator Delights and various nutrition classes through out the US. Thomas served as president for the American Heart Association in Clay County, Minnesota. Thomas is a University of Minnesota certified master gardener. Thomas was the first women and organic farmer to receive the University of Minnesota Siehl Award. Thomas and family have received Disney's highest community service award (2007) for working with over 600 children attending the Thomas family farm to learn about growing their own food. Thomas hosts "Going green on the farm" for her favorite charity the Gifted Learning Project www.giftedlearningproject.org

Photo courtesy of Sparks Magazine - Jerry Noel, Editor.

Find Out More

Seminars by the authors at Doubting Thomas Publishing are available for your business or organization. Details can be obtained by emailing us at girardsag@yahoo.com

Topics include: Nutrition for Stress busters, Heirloom gardening, Creative Learning, Overcoming obstacles and much more! Programs are tailored for your organization needs.

ACKNOWLEDGMENTS

Thank you to Lauri Winterfed-Shanks – for all of your encouragement and kindness. I am also grateful to all of the participants of Dehydrator Delight classes who encouraged me to write this book.

SOURCES
United States Department of Agriculture handbooks on nutritional values
Bowes and Church's Food Values of Portions Commonly Used, revised by Jean A.T. Pennington

COMPUTER SOURCES

Document Recreation - OfficeMax, Inc. ImPress, Dilworth, MN
Technical Director "Computer Geek" - Girard Sagmiller
Technical Support Editor - Deb Watne
Editor in Chief – Evan Thomas

PREFACE

I remember back to the taste of the dried fruit my grandmother made from fruit in her orchard. Nothing compared - not even fresh fruit. The dried fruit was so much sweeter and the room it was made in smelled like fresh apple pie. She didn't have the luxury of a food dehydrator, but used the sun and some old door screens. It was a taste filed away in my memory. Now as an adult, I enjoy that same flavor and aroma with my children.

This old form of food preservation is borrowed from our ancestors and made modern for us. The Native Americans were able to store dried foods and make it through the rough winters of the Midwest when food, especially produce, was difficult to come by. The concept of drying, although very old, is making a strong comeback. A food dehydrator is truly one of the conveniences of modern day life. **Welcome to the world of Dehydrator Delights**!

WHY A BOOK?

I have taught a number of dehydrator classes and was frustrated with the lack of good, updated drying books. This book should give you a simple, straight-forward approach to drying fruits and vegetables. I have been an avid dryer for about 8 years. About 6 tons later, I'll give you the benefit of my short cuts - and learning through my mistakes!

Since the creation of the book we have survived two natural disasters and we ate dried foods while were without electricity and heat for 2 weeks. Our family's home was an island which as surrounded by a 5 foot wall of water. Thank goodness for dried foods! You never know when you need to rely on the wisdom of planning ahead!

WHY DEHYDRATE?

Why do you want to dehydrate foods? There are many interesting responses to that question. The major reason is flavor. The foods which are rich in flavor are more intense once dried. Peaches and pineapple come to mind. They truly taste even better dried. They're one of nature's own candies, and they're a lot healthier for you. Why dehydrate?

A. The process of drying foods is controlled by you. No extra salt, preservatives, or added fats. (Some commercially available dehydrated apples contain oils that are added in the processing. Croutons made commercially sometimes contain lard.)

B. Dried fruit and vegetables are convenient to use. Snacks for brown baggers, campers, and traveling are just a few of the uses. Storage of dried foods is not a problem - no refrigeration required! An empty 4 quart plastic bucket can store the equivalent of 20-30 pounds raw apples. I have kept dried apples up to 2 years without a problem. Try storing raw ones that long!

C. There are also health reasons for drying your own fruit. The Surgeon General has stated that 35% of all cancers could be prevented through better diet. That means less fat and more fiber. Fruit and vegetables are high in fiber and low in fat (with the exception of coconut and avocado which are high in fat). Drying preserves these great characteristics. The recommended serving of fruit and vegetables is 5 a day - a tough quota to aim for, but more easily met with dried fruit and vegetables. It is easier to make this daily goal if you have the vegetables and fruit on hand and convenient, which drying does, even if the produce is out of season!

D. Dried fruits are low in sugar, cholesterol, and sodium. When I teach Dehydrator Delights as a local community education class, several of the participants have given up smoking and now purchase kitchen gadgets with the new found mad money. A food dehydrator is one of the equipment pieces gadget collectors buy. Not only have they improved their health by quitting smoking, but they have a new way to preserve food even if living alone. People living alone might actually find they have less waste. Instead of trying to use the whole onion, they can dry what they don't use for later.

Dried onion stores better than if you put a fresh onion in the refrigerator, only to find it moldy and green later.

E. In-season foods can be preserved for later use. Vidalia onions can be used and enjoyed all year round. Drying allows the product to be used at your convenience.

F. You can save the farmer's market locally grown food for use in winter when it is harder to access the great taste of fresh and local food! Especially organic food- you know they re not sprayed with chemicals banned in the US like the winter foods that come from other countries and travel GREAT DISTANCES to get to you. Local food helps local economy!

STORAGE

Storage is not much of a problem. An apartment or dorm room can easily store a lot of dried foods versus raw, frozen, or canned foods.

The truly optimum storage of dried foods is in a glass container. Glass containers have less air exchanged between the outside and the inside of container than most plastic bags. The humidity of houses differs as do the seasons and locations of your home. Humidity is reabsorbed and produces acts like a sponge if left in the open air for long periods of time or if you live in a humid area. This can mold your produce. Plastic bags work for short term, for snacks and short trips, but for long term use, glass is better.

Dried foods, spices, and herbs should be stored in a cool, dark place. I store mine in the cupboard, easily accessible for snacks, cooking, and baking. Be sure to label your products with ingredients and date. That way you'll save the current products for later and rotate your stock. Rotating your stock also may allow you to use a combination of flavors of the same product. One batch of onions may taste stronger than your previous batch, so you might want to make a comment on the label to use less. Fruits and vegetables do vary in strength of flavor, since they are agricultural products.

The fruits that are naturally sweeter I store in recycled, clean mayonnaise or jam jars. This also protects them from insects. Vegetables such as broccoli and carrots I store in thick plastic containers and they seem to keep nicely.

Be sure your product is dry before storing. To test the product, take one piece of the fruit or vegetable out of the dryer, let cool for 5 minutes, press, and touch the product. If it is done, place cooled product in a storage containers. (If you don't cool the product and it is still warm from the dehydrator, it can mold.) Ask family members to keep lids on products. Sometimes they will snack on a product and leave the lids off. The product will reabsorb some water from the air and in

WHAT DO YOU LOOK FOR IN A DEHYDRATOR?

I prefer the dehydrator that has a fan and heating element. I have seen the kind that has only a heater. Be sure if you have this kind to rotate the shelves frequently. I also like the temperature gauge on mine. It allows me to control the temperature up to 150°. In the winter when the house is a constant temperature, I might want the temperature off. On rainy summer days, I might want to have the heat at a low temperature to allow the humidity to be driven off. Or I can hurry the process by turning up the heat. Yogurt should have a temperature of about 110°. If you don't have a temperature gauge, it could be more difficult to make.

Peaches, tomatoes, and pears can be stickier than some products. I really hate to spend time cleaning something by hand. After making these, you will have to wash your dryer. Time is a commodity I have a short supply of, like all of us, so I like a product that is dishwasher safe.

I also like a good warranty. Is the warranty for parts and labor? Is it just a short period of time? Do you even have time to try it out before the warranty is up? Look for at least a 6 month warranty so you can get full use of the dryer before the warranty is up.

Routinely check the temperature of your dehydrator if it has a heating element. A participant in a class of mine had the misfortune of burning all of her products. She rotated the trays frequently and still burned her produce. After discussing it with her later, I asked her to check the temperature of the dryer with a thermometer. Sure enough, the thermostat was defective. Routinely check your dehydrator. They do vary just like ovens do from household to household.

5 Precautions and Caveats:

1. Dried food is harder, and like peanuts, can present a choking hazard if you have small children, especially if they like to run around while eating.

2. Be sure to brush and floss as normal dental hygiene since leathers and dried fruit do contain natural sugars which can stick to teeth.

3. Also, if you do choose to use honey in recipes, do not serve the product to children under the age of 1. Honey should not be fed to children under the age of 1 because of botulism spores.

4. Meat and poultry should be cooked to reach an internal temperature of 1600 before making beef or turkey jerky. A food bacterium in meat is not killed in the dryer and food poisoning can result if you are using raw meat.
(Courtesy of USDA Meat and Poultry Hotline).

5. Do not dry flowers in the dehydrator you use for food. Commercially purchased flowers have been sprayed for insects and fungus. The sprays can be absorbed in the dehydrator and cause contamination of your food products. I use a separate inexpensive dehydrator for flowers.

ELECTRICITY

Most dehydrators do not use that much electricity, especially since you only do the process once and don't have the extended use of electricity as with a freezer or refrigerator.

The dehydrator manufacture can give an accurate amount of kilowatts used by the dehydrator in an hour. Call your electric company to get the latest price of kilowatts. You can keep track of hours used on the dehydrator and figure the price of your product.

I like to use a surge protector on the outlets. It will protect your electrical equipment from large surges of electricity.

To figure your cost of dried food, here is a formula:

- Cost of KLW (check your local utility company for rates) (based on one KLW usage per hour) X hours it took you to dry the food.

- Plus the initial cost of the food.

- Then divide the number by the weight of the food (usually in ounces) = the cost of the food.

Example: Apples were purchased at $0.79 a pound. 2 pounds were purchased and my kilowatts are 3.5 cents per hour.

      3.5 (cost of KLW) X 10 hours it took to dry the food. = .35
      + (.79 X 2 pounds of apples) = $1.93
      $1.93 - 6 ounces = .32 per ounce is the cost of dried food

Drying food you really do save compared to commercially available dried foods. The cost is even less if you have a garden or fruit tree.

SAVING MONEY

Does food drying save money? Yes, if you can purchase foods on sale and in season and then dry them for later use. Dried spices and herbs from your garden or window box can be a huge savings. The tastes of these are far more superior also.

Does it always save you money? I would honestly have to say "no" in some cases. Potato chips can easily be cheaper on sale than making apple chips, but nutritionally, the two are very far apart (see next page for comparison). I also find that with dried foods, we eat a lot more produce. One lug of peaches does not last us a year. It is not uncommon for us to go through 3 lugs when we would not have eaten 3 lugs of raw peaches in season. I can dry the peaches instead of trying to can the fruit, which is much more time consuming and dangerous with small, active children around.

Suitability for Drying

Table 1, shows what is suitable for drying. Tables are by the University of Florida.

Table 1. Fruits At A Glance

Fruit	Suitability For Drying	Suitability For Fruit Leather	Fruit	Suitability For Drying	Suitability For Fruit Leather
Apples	Excellent	Excellent	Guavas	Not recommended[5]	Only in combination
Apricots	Excellent	Excellent	Melons	Poor	Not recommended
Avocados	Not recommended[1]	Not recommended	Nectarines	Excellent	Excellent
Bananas	Good	Fair to good	Olives	Not recommended[6]	Not recommended
Berries with seeds	Not recommended[2]	Excellent	Papayas	Good	Better in combination
Blueberries	Fair	Poor unless in combination	Peaches	Excellent	Excellent
Cherries	Excellent	Excellent	Pears	Excellent	Excellent
Citrus fruits	Not recommended[3]	Only in combination	Persimmons	Fair	Not recommended
Citrus peel	Excellent	Only in combination	Pineapples	Excellent	Excellent
Coconuts	Excellent	Only in combination	Plums	Good	Good
Crabapples	Not recommended[4]	Only in combination	Pomegranates	Not recommended[7]	Not recommended
Cranberries	Poor	Only in combination	Prune plums	Excellent	Excellent
Currants	Good	Not recommended	Quince	Not recommended[8]	Not recommended
Dates	Excellent	Only in combination	Rhubarb	Good[9]	Fair
Figs	Excellent	Only in combination	Strawberries	Fair to good	Excellent
Grapes	Excellent	Fair to good			

1. High fat content.
2. High seed content and slow rate of drying.
3. Too juicy and pulp lacks firm texture.
4. Too small and tart; can be combined with other fruit for leather.
5. Grainy flesh full of seeds; combine with other fruit for leather.
6. High oil content. Bitter flavor removable only by long processing.
7. Pulp is full of seeds.
8. Hard flesh and strongly acidic flavor. Combine with other fruit for leather.
9. **Never** consume leaves-they contain toxic salts of oxalic acid.

Drying Fruits At Home

Table 2. Drying Fruits At Home

Fruit	Preparation	Pretreatment (Choose One)				Drying Times Dehydrator (hours)
		Sulfur (hours)	Blanch		Other	
			Steam (minutes)	Syrup (minutes)		
Apples	Peel and core, cut into slices or rings about 1/8-inch thick.	¾	3-5 (depending on texture)	10	-ascorbic acid solution -ascorbic acid mixture -fruit juice dip -sulfite dip	6-12
Apricots	Pit and halve. May slice if desired.	2	3-4	10	-ascorbic acid solution -ascorbic acid mixture -fruit juice dip -sulfite dip	24-36**
Bananas	Use solid yellow or slightly brown-flecked bananas. Avoid bruised or overripe bananas. Peel and slice ¼-inch to 1/8-inch thick, crosswise or lengthwise.				-honey dip -ascorbic acid solution -ascorbic acid mixture -fruit juice dip -sulfite dip	8-10
Berries Firm:	Wash and drain berries. With waxy coating - blueberries, cranberries, currants, gooseberries, huckleberries.				-Plunge into boiling water 15-30 seconds to "check" skins. Stop cooking action by placing fruit in ice water. Drain on paper towels. -No treatment necessary.	24-36
Soft:	Boysenberries and strawberries					24-36
Cherries	Stem, wash, drain, and pit fully ripe cherries. Cut in half, chop or leave whole.			10 (for sour cherries)	-Whole-dip in boiling water 30 seconds or more to "check" skins. -Cut and pitted:no treatment necessary.	24-36

Table 2. Drying Fruits At Home

Fruit	Preparation	Pretreatment (Choose One)				Drying Times Dehydrator (hours)[1]
		Sulfur (hours)	Blanch		Other	
			Steam (minutes)	Syrup (minutes)		
Citrus peel	Peels of citron, grapefruit, kumquat, lime, lemon, tangelo and tangerine can be dried. Thick-skinned navel orange peel dries better than thin-skinned Valencia peel. Wash thoroughly. Remove outer 1/6-to 1/8-inch of peel. Avoid white bitter pith.				-No pretreatment	8-12
Figs	Select fully ripe fruit. Immature fruit may sour before drying. Wash or clean whole fruit with damp cloth. Leave small fruit whole, otherwise cut in half.	1 (whole)			-Whole:Dip in boiling water 30 seconds or more to "check" skins. Plunge in ice water to stop further cooking. Drain on paper towels.	6-12"
Grapes Seedless:	Leave whole				-Whole:Dip in boiling water 30 seconds or more to "check" skins. Plunge in ice water to stop further cooking. Drain on paper towels. -Halves:No treatment necessary.	12-20
With Seeds:	-Cut in half and remove seeds					
Nectarines and Peaches	When sulfuring, pit and halve, if desired, remove skins. For steam and syrup blanching, leave whole, then pit and halve. May also be sliced or quartered.	2-3 (halves) 1 (slices)	8	10	-ascorbic acid solution -ascorbic acid mixture -fruit juice dip -sulfiting	36-48"

11

Table 2. Drying Fruits At Home

| Fruit | Preparation | Pretreatment (Choose One) | | | | Drying Times Dehydrator (hours)* |
| | | Sulfur (hours) | Blanch | | Other | |
			Steam (minutes)	Syrup (minutes)		
Pears	Cut in half and core. Peeling preferred. May also slice or quarter.	5 (halves) 2 (slices)	6 (halves)	10	-ascorbic acid solution -ascorbic acid mixture -fruit juice dip -sulfiting	24-36"
Persimmons	Use firm fruit of long, soft varieties or fully ripe fruit of round drier varieties. Peel and slice using stainless steel knife.				-may syrup blanch	12-15"
Pineapple	Use fully ripe, fresh pineapple. Wash, peel and remove thorny eyes. Slice lengthwise and remove core. Cut in ½-inch slices. crosswise.				-No treatment necessary	24-36
Plums (Prunes)	Leave whole or if sulfuring, halve the fruit.	1			-Sun drying:(whole) dip in boiling water 30 seconds or more to "check" skins. -Oven or dehydrator drying:rinse in hot tap water.	24-36"

* Because of variations in air circulation, drying times in conventional ovens could be up to twice as long. Drying times for sun drying could range from 2 to 6 days. depending on temperature and humidity.

** Drying times are shorter for slices and other cuts of fruit.

COMPARISON OF HOMEMADE APPLE CHIPS AND POTATO CHIPS

Dried Apple Chips   vs.   Potato Chips

1 ounce (1\3 cup)   1 ounce (one
small bag)

Calories- 69 calories   Calories- 148
calories
Fat- 0.1 grams   Fat- 10.0 grams
Sodium- 0.3 mg   Sodium- 133.2
mg

See bar graph on next page.

BAR GRAPHS

The bar graphs compare sodium, cholesterol, fat, and calories of Dehydrator Delights recipes to name brand products. The difference is amazing. See for yourself!

SODIUM MILLIGRAMS

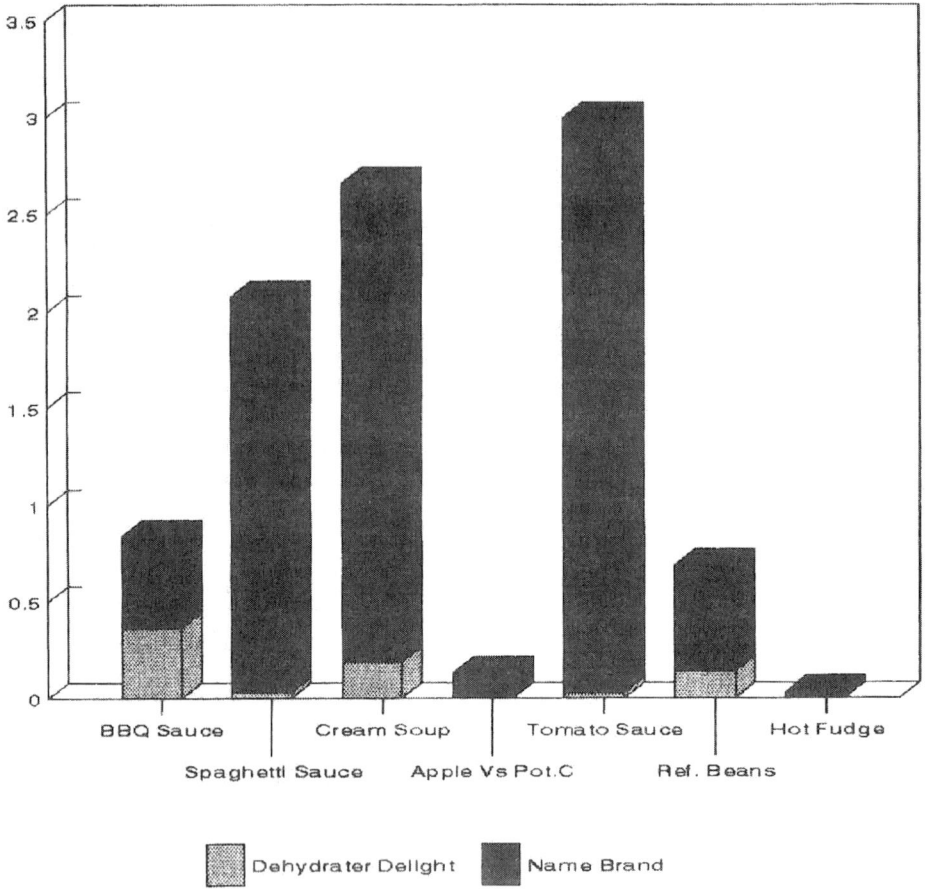

Legend: Dehydrater Delight, Name Brand

Categories: BBQ Sauce, Spaghetti Sauce, Cream Soup, Apple Vs Pot.C, Tomato Sauce, Ref. Beans, Hot Fudge

FAT GRAMS

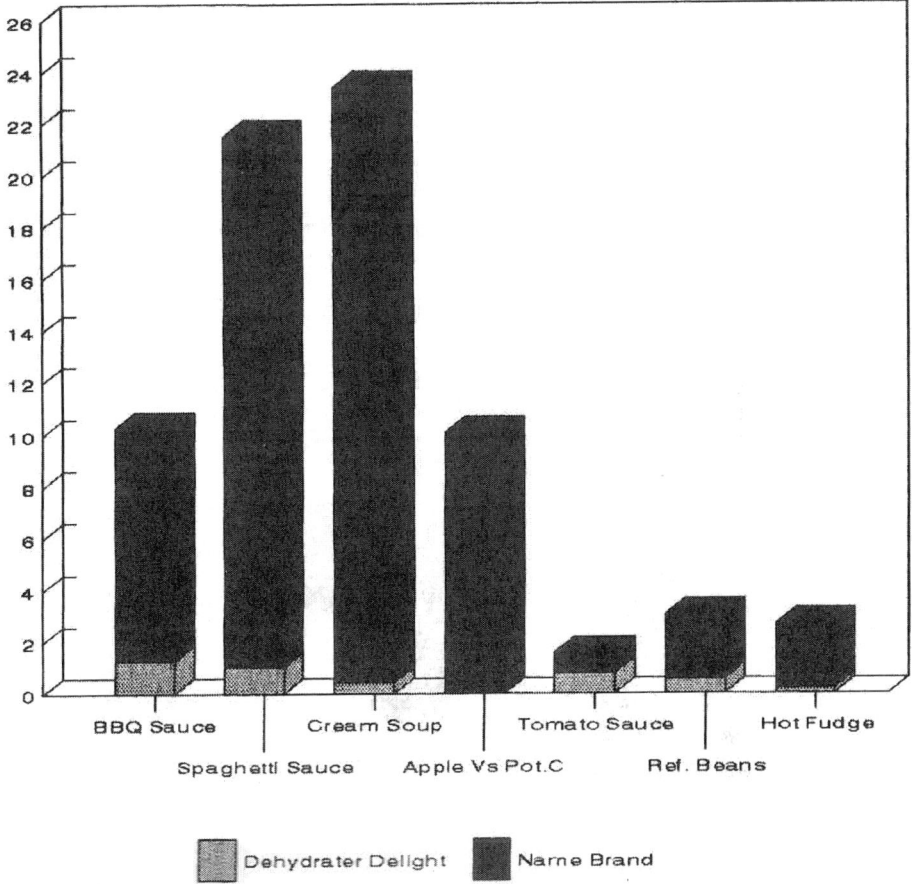

Chart categories (x-axis): BBQ Sauce, Spaghetti Sauce, Cream Soup, Apple Vs Pot.C, Tomato Sauce, Ref. Beans, Hot Fudge

Legend: Dehydrater Delight, Narne Brand

Y-axis: 0, 2, 4, 6, 8, 10, 12, 14, 16, 18, 20, 22, 24, 26

15

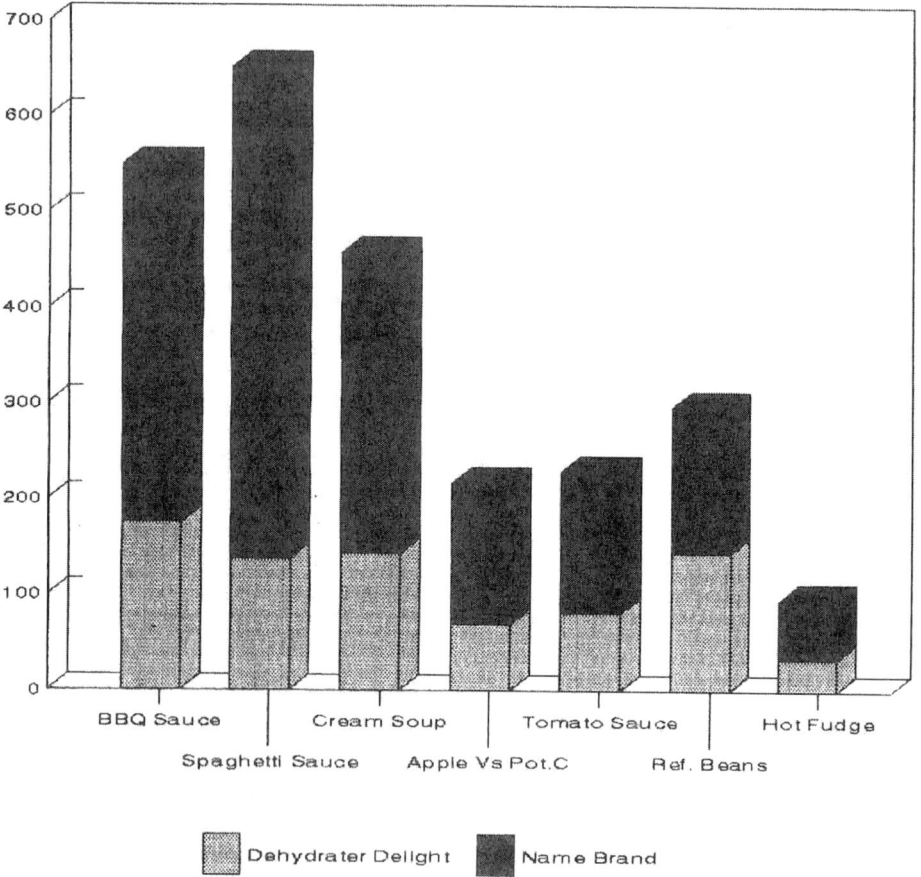

CALORIES

Legend: Dehydrater Delight, Name Brand

Categories: BBQ Sauce, Spaghetti Sauce, Cream Soup, Apple Vs Pot.C, Tomato Sauce, Ref. Beans, Hot Fudge

CHOLESTEROL MILLIGRAMS

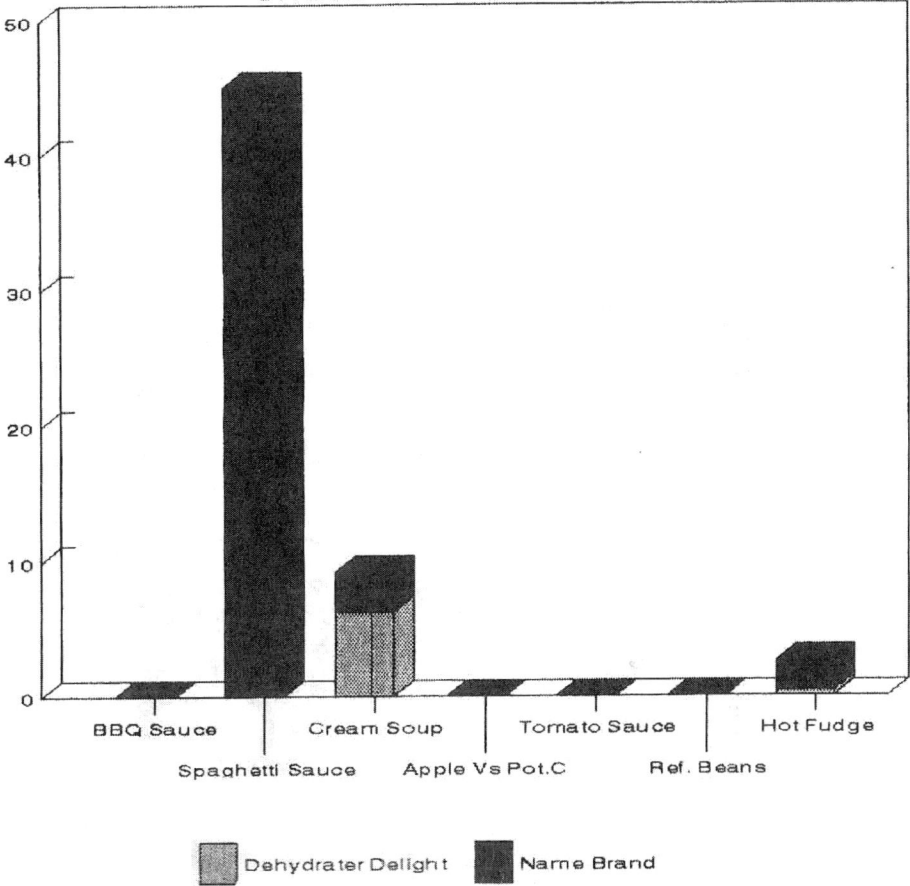

BBQ Sauce	Cream Soup	Tomato Sauce	Hot Fudge
Spaghetti Sauce	Apple Vs Pot.C	Ref. Beans	

Dehydrater Delight   Name Brand

Dehydrator Delights BBQ Sauce 2 cups 175 calories 1.3 g fat 367 mg sodium 0 mg cholesterol	Vs	Name Brand BBQ Sauce 2 cups 375 calories 9.0 g fat 4075 mg sodium 0 mg cholesterol
Dehydrator Delights Spaghetti Sauce 2 cups 87 calories 1 g fat 32.1 mg sodium 0 mg cholesterol	Vs	Name Brand Spaghetti Sauce w/ Meatballs 2 cups 515 calories 20.5 g fat 2440 mg sodium 45 mg cholesterol
Dehydrator Delights Cream Mushroom Soup 1 can 143 calories .4 g fat 189.7 mg sodium 6.2 mg cholesterol	Vs	Name Brand Cream Mushroom Soup 1 can 314 calories 23 g fat 2470.5 mg sodium 3.0 mg cholesterol

Dehydrator Delights Dried Apple Chips 1 ounce (1\3 cup) 69 calories 0.1 g fat 0.3 mg sodium	Vs.	Name Brand Potato Chips 1 ounce (one small bag) 148 calories 10.0 g fat 133.2 mg sodium
Dehydrator Delights Tomato Sauce 81 calories 0.8 g fat 29.9 mg sodium 0 mg cholesterol	Vs.	Name Brand Tomato Sauce 147 calories 0.8 g fat 2964.5 mg sodium 0 mg cholesterol
Dehydrator Delights Refried Beans 144 calories 0.6 g fat 138 mg sodium 0 mg cholesterol	Vs.	Name Brand Refried Beans 153 calories 2.5 g fat 541 mg sodium 0 mg cholesterol
Dehydrator Delights Hot Fudge Sauce 1 tablespoon 33 calories 0.2 g fat 13.5 mg sodium 0.4 mg cholesterol	Vs.	Name Brand Hot Fudge Sauce 1 tablespoon 62 calories 2.5 g fat 21.5 mg sodium 2.2 mg cholesterol

LOW FAT - How to Section

Produce should be always washed and "spots" and bruises cut off. Always blot produce dry; removing this added moisture decreases the drying time. No pretreatment of produce is required. Sulfuring, blanching, etc., seems a waste of time, and spoils some of the nutritional value, so I don't do blanching or sulfuring.

The humidity and temperature of your home and climate greatly impact the drying times. Other contributing factors that vary drying times are the size of dryer, heat temperature, and size of the produce slices. Thinner slices will dry faster than thick ones. The drying times are approximate based on temperatures of 90-105°.

Fruits and vegetables of different varieties may be dehydrated at the same time with the exception of onions, garlic, and peppers. Clean the trays with lemon juice after using onion, garlic or pepper. This will eliminate cross-contamination. Moist produce such as tomatoes or leather should be dried on the lower trays in case of dripping onto another tray.

Dried produce should be tested by removing a piece of the produce from the dehydrator, letting it cool for 5 minutes, then touching and pressing it to see if it feels moist. If the product is very sticky, chances are the produce is not dry yet. Let the product cool before placing it in containers, as it is still usually warm (if you have a heater unit) and can mold easily if not allowed to cool for 5-7 minutes before placing in a glass container.

Slices can be placed anywhere on the tray as long as the slices do not overlap. Don't worry about arranging neatly on the tray, the slices will pull away from each other as they dry.

When reconstituting fruit and vegetables, refrigerate if longer than 1 hour to prevent bacteria growth.

Leathers can be made from any combination of foods you like. Line the tray with microwaveable plastic or use a tray that is made for leathers. If lining the tray with plastic wrap, use masking tape and tape the sides of plastic to the tray.

The recipes included in this book are low in fat and cholesterol. Be cautious of other books that use the goodness of dried produce mixed in a recipe with high fat ingredients.

FRUIT SECTION WITH LOW FAT AND RECIPES

APPLES

Optimum temperature for drying fruits is 130° to 135°.

Dry the apples with skin on or off. If you plan on using the apples in a recipe, take the skin off. Wash apples, cut off bruises, core, and slice. I like to use the corer, peeler, slicer purchased at a kitchen gadget store. The kids and I work together and can easily belt out 30 pounds of apples ready to dehydrate in 45 minutes. The apple rinds can be boiled with water to remove any odors in your household and even works on fish odors!

Dry 6-12 hours. Apples are dry if pressed and the apple breaks apart cleanly without tearing. Dried apple should not feel moist and feels like dry leather. Eat as snack or use in trail mix. To reconstitute, cover with water and let set 30-60 minutes until soft. You may use in place of raw apple in recipes but add a little more liquid to the recipe. Add 1 /4 cup extra water with the reconstituted apples when making apple crisp or pie.

Variations of dried apples:

- Sprinkle lightly with cinnamon and sugar (no more than ½ tablespoon per tray) before drying, and then dehydrate. This tastes like apple pie without the hassle of preparing apple pie and doesn't contain all the calories (and fat) from the crust. You can also use sugar substitute for those watching carbs.
- Sprinkle lightly with dry Jell-O (1 teaspoon per 12 apple slices) straight from the box.
- Dip in pineapple or orange juice; the flavor will be different and apples will not brown as much as regular method.

Low fat cooking tip

Use this applesauce instead of oil in baking and cooking. (It even works for brownies.) If recipe calls for 1 \4 cup oil or shortening or margarine just substitutes equal portions of the applesauce. The applesauce increases the fiber and nutrients, and decreases the fat in the recipe, and you will not taste the applesauce at all!

APPLESAUCE FROM DRIED APPLES 1 serving

1\2 cup dried apples
1\2 cup water
dash of cinnamon and nutmeg

Soak apples in water for 20 minutes. Blend well in food processor or blender. If the apples are tart then use sugar to sweeten. Add dash of lemon juice if you would like the applesauce not to brown.

1 serving   =   105 calories Approximate 0.2g fat
Value   0.5 mgs sodium
                   0 mg cholesterol

APPLESAUCE LEATHER

Pour commercial unsweetened applesauce or homemade applesauce on plastic lined (or fruit leather) tray 1 \4 inch thick. Dry 12-18 hours till pliable and not sticky. For homemade applesauce use apples that are cored, peeled, and sliced. Blend apples with dash of cinnamon, nutmeg, and sugar (if needed) and teaspoon of lemon juice. Pour on tray 1 \4 inch thick. Applesauce can be mixed with equal amounts of pears, berries, or bananas.

DEHYDRATOR DELIGHT APPLE CAKE (Serves 9)

 2\3 cup applesauce
1\2 cup sugar
2 egg whites
1 tablespoon vanilla
1 teaspoon baking powder (prefer low sodium) 1\2 tablespoon
    cinnamon
1 cup all purpose flour
1 \2 whole wheat flour
1\2 cup dried (reconstitute) apples (or 1 cup fresh apple)

In large bowl, mix applesauce, sugar, egg whites, vanilla, baking
powder, baking soda, cinnamon, and flour. Mix well, and then add
rehydrated apples. Pour in 9x9 pan. Bake at 350 for 30 minutes.

1 serving   =   145 calories Approximate 0.3g fat
Value   12.3 mgs sodium
                 0 mgs cholesterol

APPLES AND BREAD

(LOW FAT AND LOW CHOLESTEROL) (Serves 12) 1 loaf thawed
frozen bread (prefer whole wheat)
1 \2 cup dried apples
1 tablespoon each of cinnamon and nutmeg
3 tablespoons sugar
1 \3 cup raisins (if desired)

Reconstitute apples in 1 cup water for 20 minutes. Drain. Roll out
thawed, frozen bread. Place reconstituted apples on bread. Sprinkle
cinnamon, sugar, nutmeg, and raisins over bread evenly. Roll up
and let rise in pan. Bake at 350 for 25 minutes until done.

1 serving	=	124 calories
Approximate		1g fat
Value		200.2 mgs sodium
(Without raisins)		0 mgs cholesterol

APRICOTS

These do not look or taste like store bought apricots. Apricots will be
browner and harder than store bought. (Store bought ones is made
with sulfur to preserve them this can cause migraines in some
people or allergic reactions.) Wash apricots, pit, and slice in ¼ inch
pieces. Dry 15-25 hours. The apricots will be fairly hard but will
bend once pressed. Reconstitute 1-2 hours in enough water to cover
the apricots (refrigerate while reconstituting).

HOT FRUIT DESSERT (Serves 14)

10 halves dried apricots (can use peaches or apples)
10 pitted prunes
1-20 oz can pineapple chunks (light syrup or water packed), drained
1-12 oz can fruit cocktail (prefer the light syrup), drained
1\4 cup water

Place apricots and prunes in large cake pan 12x8x2. Combine other ingredients and spoon over dried fruit. Bake uncovered at 350 for 50-60 minutes. Serve warm.

1 serving	=	238 calories
Approximate		0.5 g fat
Value		6.8 mgs sodium
		0 mgs cholesterol

APRICOT PUDDING OR PIE FILLING (Serves 8)

10 halves dried apricot slices
¼ cup raisins
1 box vanilla pudding (not instant) - 7 ounce package
3 cups skim milk (2 cups milk for pie filling)
dash cinnamon

Place ¼ cup apricot slices in saucepan, add 4-5 dried plums, and ¼ cup raisins. Add vanilla pudding mixture (not instant, use cook 'n serve). Pour 2 cups skim milk and stir constantly until mixture thickens and pudding is done. Sprinkle with cinnamon and serve warm.

1 serving	=	146 calories
Approximate		0.2 g fat
Value		202.6 mgs sodium
		1.6 mgs cholesterol

BANANAS

Bananas for banana chips should be used before they start to brown. If the bananas are very ripe, use for fruit leather. Banana chips are good in trail mix. The banana chips without dip will be browner and will bend once pressed. If you would like them to not be as brown, dip in orange juice and slice thin. Dry 12-30 hours until crisp. To reconstitute, cover ½ cup banana with 1 cup water, 1-2 hours, in refrigerator. If chips are too strong tasting and very brown, try using less ripe bananas.

LEATHERS

½ cup raw banana or ½ cup applesauce (homemade or store-bought)

½ cup strawberries, or blueberries or huckleberries, or raspberries,

Dash of cinnamon

Blend all ingredients in blender, then pour ¼ inch thick on plastic wrap lined trays or trays made for leather making. Dried leather when done should be shiny on bottom and pull away from sides of tray. Leather should not be moist to touch. Use pizza cutter and cutting board to cut leather in desired shapes or rectangles. Drying time is usually 12-19 hour s. Store bought banana chips are coated with honey. If you like that type of chip, try dipping banana slices in mixture of ½ cup pineapple juice and ½ cup honey. Place on tray and dehydrate 10-15 hours until crisp.

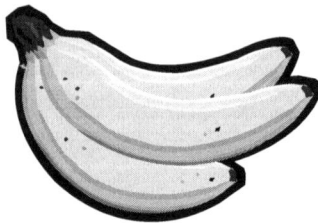

FRUITY BREAKFAST SHAKES (Serves 1)

1 \4 cup dried pineapple or fresh
1 \3 teaspoon sugar
1 cup skim milk
dash cinnamon

Place handful of banana chips in blender, then add rest of
   ingredients. Blend well.

Approximate = 116 calories
Value Based < I gram of fat
On Fresh   127.1 mgs sodium
Fruit   4.4 mgs cholesterol

BERRIES - Strawberries, Huckleberries, June berries, and

Blueberries.

Dry 14-30 hours. Wash, hull, slice ¼ inch thick, and place on tray. I
use an egg cutter to slice my berries, and then cut my drying time
to 8-14 hours. Dried strawberries will resemble and feel like bright
red ground corn cereal. Dried berries are fun to put in trail mix, but
I do prefer to use berries with banana or applesauce in making fruit
leather. The berry leathers made just with berries are seedy and
hard to chew. For recipes, reconstitute 1-2 hours or overnight in
refrigerator. Sauces and fruit crisps can be made with reconstituted
berries. Dried berries are good in cooked cereal, pancakes, waffles,
muffins, and trail mix.

BERRY GOOD SAUCE (Makes about 3 cups)

1 tablespoon lemon juice
2 tablespoons cornstarch
1\4 cup sugar
3\4 cup-1 cup water or liquid from rehydrated berries
2 cups rehydrated blueberries, or strawberries

In 1 quart casserole stir ingredients together. Put the microwave on
high for 10-25 minutes until thick. Stir every 7-10 minutes.

POWERED SUGAR STARWBERRIES

Clean and hull berries. Cut into slices. Roll in powdered sugar lightly. Dry 16-20 hours. Tastes just like candy!

BERRY LEATHER

1 cup of berries (strawberries or blueberries etc.) 1 cup mashed
    banana
dash of cinnamon

Wash berries and peel banana to equal 1 cup. Blend together and pour ¼ inch thick on lined tray. Dry 12-19 hours. You should be able to roll leather out of tray without sticking. If unable to do this, turn leather over and dehydrate until it is not sticky or moist. Should feel like leather (i. e. soft leather shoes).

1 serving =	(based on raw strawberries)
Complete	187 calories
Recipe	1.1 g fat
Approximate	10.2 mgs sodium Value
	0 mgs cholesterol

CHERRIES

Wash, pit, and slice cherries. Dry 20-35 hours. Great as snack, in desserts, or in quick breads. Cherries should not feel moist when dehydrated. Reconstitute by soaking in water to cover cherries overnight or 1-2 hours in refrigerator.

CITRUS (Oranges, grapefruit, tangerines, lemon)

The easiest way to dry citrus is to use a serrated grapefruit spoon and dig out citrus fruit (as if you were going to eat a grapefruit). The fruit will come out of the peel in sections and this way you are not drying the membranes that can be hard. Place sections on dehydrator and dry for 18-35 hours. The citrus can also be cut into thin slices and dried. Wash citrus peels before drying. Take the peel off before eating. Works for lemons as well. The dried lemon slices can be used in ice tea or water for a great refresher. Orange slices can be used in craft items or potpourri. Reconstitute 2 hours in water in refrigerator.

ORANGE SLICE PORK CHOPS

4 lean pork chops-
1 teaspoon low sodium chicken bouillon
2\3 cup boiling water
6 slices dried orange or 1 fresh orange, cut in slices
2 teaspoons prepared mustard
Optional - pepper to taste

Trim fat from chops. Place chops in 4 quart casserole dish. Dissolve bouillon cubes in hot water, add mustard, and pour over chops. Place slices of dried orange under and over the chops. Cover and place in oven at 350° for 45-55 minutes. Spoon liquid over chops every 15 minutes until thoroughly cooked.

1 serving =	232 calories
Approximate	10 g fat
Value	103 mgs sodium
	83.3 mgs cholesterol

LEMONS APPLE MUFFINS (12 servings)

3 egg whites
½ cup skim milk
¼ cup applesauce
2 tablespoons lemon juice
1 /4 cup powdered lemons (skin removed) or ¼ cup raw lemon,
    ground up
¾ cup flour
½ cup brown sugar
1 /2 teaspoon baking powder (low sodium)
2 teaspoons cinnamon
¼ teaspoon nutmeg
½ cup chopped apple (raw)

Preheat over to 400°. Mix moist ingredients together. Set aside. Mix dry ingredients together. Add dry to moist until all is moist, but lumpy. Spoon into greased tin or paper-lined muffin tin. Bake 20 min.

1 serving   =   69 calories
Approximate   0.2 g fat
Value   20.8 mgs sodium
                 0.2 mgs cholesterol

CRANBERRIES

Cranberries can be dried but do take a long time to dry whole. Cut the berries in half or process in food processor. Spread mixture evenly 1 \4 inch or less in lined tray. Dry 12-20 hours until you can peel leather off tray. Reconstitute by adding equal amounts of apple juice. Soak overnight or 1-2 days in refrigerator.

CRANBERRY FRUIT LEATHER

1 cup fresh clean cranberries

1 orange peeled removed

1 cup unsweetened applesauce ½ teaspoon of cinnamon

Blend or process ingredients together still smooth. Pour onto plastic lined or leather making trays 1\4 inch thick or less. Dry until leather pulls away from sides - 8-14 hours.

1 serving =	218 calories
Total Recipe	0.8 g fat
Approximate	9.3 mgs sodium
Value	0 mgs cholesterol

CRANBERRY SAUCE (Serves 4)

1 \2 cup sugar
1\4 cup water
1 cup dried reconstituted cranberries (or ½ cup raw) dash of
    cinnamon

In 4 quart casserole stir sugar, water, and dried cranberries. Cover. Microwave on high 10 minutes; stir. Microwave for 15-20 minutes until thick. Serve warm or chill. You may add ground-up orange to mixture also for variety. Heat additional 3-5 minutes.

1 serving =	102 calories
Approximate	< 1 g fat
Value	0.4 mgs sodium
0 mgs cholesterol	

GRAPES

Dried grapes or raisins are truly sweeter than store bought. Store bought are usually coated with a lubricant to keep them from sticking together. Raisins that you make from whole grapes will take you up to 40 hours to make. To cut down on drying time, remove from stem, rinse and slice grapes with a processor. Place on trays and dry 16-24 hours. White, green, or purple work fine - just make sure they are seedless! Raisins will be a little sticky, but harder than store bought. Dried grapes should not feel moist. You may also use as mincemeat. Rehydration is not necessary unless you would like to add to breads; then soak 15-30 minutes.

DRIED GRAPE STUFFING FOR CHOPS

1 cup (reconstituted) dry apples
1 \4 cup dried grapes or raisins
2 egg whites beaten
1\2 teaspoon cinnamon
1 \8 black pepper

In mixing bowl combine ingredients and divide between pork chops. May add butter substitute-1 teaspoon to mixture.

1 serving = 87.8 calories
Total Recipe   0.1 g fat
Approximate   26.5 mgs sodium
Value   0 mgs cholesterol

RAISIN FILLING FOR COOKIES

¾ cup sugar

½ cup water

1 lb. raisins (3-4 cups dried grapes)

Cook until thick, use in recipe for "filled" cookies. Can also use dried peaches, apricots, or nectarines. Mix with oatmeal and cook for a camping trip or morning breakfast.

RAISIN SAUCE (Yields 2 cups)
1 /4 cup raisins
2 cups water
1 cup brown sugar
2 tablespoons cornstarch
¼ teaspoon ginger
1 tablespoon vinegar

Combine raisins with water. Simmer 5 minutes. Combine other ingredients. Simmer until thick.

Per tablespoon = 22 calories
Approximate   0 g fat
Value   1.5 mgs sodium
                    0 mgs cholesterol

KIWI

Take skin off of kiwi, slice thin and dry 16-40 hours. Kiwi are wonderful in trail mix or as snack. The green color adds interest to fruit salad. Reconstitute 20 minutes with water to cover dried kiwi. They are better eaten as dried.

KIWI FRUIT SALAD (Yields 40 servings)

½ cup dried kiwi or 2 large fresh 2 cups banana
1 teaspoon lemon juice
1 cup fresh or frozen blueberries ½ cup maple syrup
1 cup water

Blend together. Serve over waffles on pancakes. May heat also.

Per tablespoon = 25 calories
Approximate   0 g fat
Value   0.9 mgs sodium
                      0 mgs cholesterol

MELONS (Cantaloupe, Watermelon)
Melons should not be over ripe or smell fermented. Cut flesh part of melon away from rind. Slice into ¼ inch pieces and dry 19-35 hours. Eat as is. Reconstituted really is not a desirable product. (You may want to place on clear plastic wrap lined trays as the watermelon tends to be sticky.)

PEACHES AND NECTARINES
Wash outside of produce. DON'T BOTHER TAKING SKIN OFF OR BLANCHING. Slice into 1 /4 inch slices with skin on and put on trays. Dry 24-35 hours. Dried peaches/nectarines do not feel moist to touch but will be bendable. The produce will darken a bit but it does not bother the flavor. These are a big favorite. You can use already canned peaches. Strain canned peaches and place on tray until dry. Reconstitute in orange juice 1-2 hours in refrigerator.

NOTE: If the peaches have dark places on the peach once dried - the taste is still good, just use in fillings for cookies or bars.

Peach Pie

3 C. dried peaches
3 C. boiling water
2/3 C. flour
1 C. sugar
2 t. cinnamon
1/4 t. nutmeg

Cover fruit with water and let soak for 30 minutes. Simmer and add sugar, spices and flour to thicken. Pour into pie crust, dot with butter, and cover with pie top. Bake at 400 F for 30 minutes

PEACH CRISP (Serves 12)
1 cup reconstituted dry peaches (or 1 cup raw)
1 package cake mix, yellow (dry)
1\2 cup applesauce
1 teaspoon cinnamon
Optional - 1 \2 cup Nutty Grits (generic term for high fiber nutty type cereal)

Mix ingredients together. Bake at 325° for 50 minutes.

1 serving =	191 calories
Approximate	3 g fat
Value	290.5 mgs sodium
(Without	0 mgs cholesterol
Nutty Grits)	

PEARS

Wash and take skin off. Slice into 1 \4 inch thick pieces and place on trays. Dried pears will be leathery but will bend when pressed. Dry 10-16 hours. Pears will be grainy as they have a high content of fiber. Eat as snack or reconstitute by covering with water for 1 hour.

PEAR OATMEAL (1 serving)

1\4 cup dried pear (or ½ cup raw)
1 1 \2 cups water
1 \4 cup water (soak pear in and then drain after reconstituting pear)
2\3 cup old-fashioned oatmeal (steel cut oatmeal is the best- better fiber and better nutrients)

Put ingredients in saucepan. Heat until mixture boils. Reduce heat and simmer until pears are soft.

1 serving =	157.6 calories
Approximate	2 g fat
Value	1 mg sodium
	0 mgs cholesterol

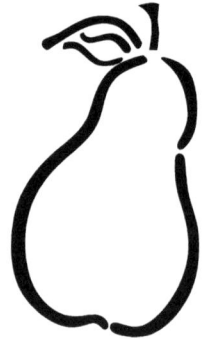

PEAR REFRESHER (Serves 2)

1\2 cup reconstituted dry pear (or ½ raw)
1\2 cup orange juice
1banana
1 cup ice cubes
1 cup low sodium seltzer

Place ingredients except seltzer in blender. Blend well.
Pour into 2 tall glasses. Pour 1 \2 cup seltzer in each glass. Serve.

1 serving =	105 calories
Approximate	0.6 g fat
Value	26 mgs sodium

PINEAPPLE

Use fresh or canned pineapple. Slice pineapple into 1 \4 inch thick slices. Place on tray and dry 2460 hours. Dry until not sticky and feels leathery. Pineapple chips purchased in the stores are usually coated with honey and are more brittle. Home dried pineapple is bendable and will be naturally sweet. They will be great to eat as is or in trail mix. Reconstitute in water for 20 minutes.

SWEET AND SOUR SAUCE FOR STIR FRY (Serves 4)

3 tablespoons cider vinegar
3 tablespoons brown sugar
6 ounces tomato sauce-low sodium or homemade
1\4 cup dried pineapple or 1\2 cup fresh
1 tablespoon powdered onion

Mix ingredients together, and gently simmer in frying pan. Add leftover, lean, cooked meat, frozen vegetables, and heat till mixture is hot. Serve over yolkless noodles or steamed rice.

1 serving =	54 calories
Approximate	0.2 g fat
Value	7.9 mgs sodium
	0 mgs cholesterol

RHUBARB

One grocery bag dries down to fit into 1 cup! You will wonder if someone switched dehydrators on you! Clean and cut rhubarb. Place on trays and dry 12-19 hours. Dried rhubarb will resemble dried chunks of grass clippings. To rehydrate, cover with water for 20 minutes. Rhubarb will not be completely like the raw state. Best in sauces, bars, or cakes.

RHUBARB AND STRAWBERRY LEATHER

1 cup rhubarb cut up

1 cup strawberries (fresh)

May add 1 tablespoon strawberry gelatin. Blend ingredients together. Pour 1 \4 inch thick on plastic wrapped lined trays or leather-making trays. Leather will be done when it starts to pull away from tray sides. Dry 12-19 hours.

Total leather = Approximate Value	71 calories
	0.8 g fat
	6.8 mgs sodium
	0 mgs cholesterol

RHUBARB SAUCE

3 cups reconstituted rhubarb
1\2 cup sugar
1\2 cup raw, cut up strawberries

Combine ingredients in a saucepan; cook slowly until fruit is tender.

Serve over fresh fruit like banana or add to plain yogurt. A great topping for vanilla ice milk.

VEGETABLES SECTION AND LOW FAT/LOW CHOLESTEROL RECIPES

Optimum temperature for drying vegetables is 1300 to 135°.

ASPARAGUS

Use only young, tender asparagus! I made the mistake of drying over mature stalks. I made a casserole from the overripe, dried asparagus when by chance, my brother-in-law popped in for lunch. He and my husband were in business together at the time. The casserole was tough and barely palatable. My brother-in-law politely choked it down. The next day he decided to quit the business and move to Montana. He did not come to our house for lunch until 3 years later. To this day I blame the casserole with that old tough asparagus!

Dry 1\4 inch thick slices, clean, tender stalks 24-40 hours. Best used in soups that requires a long cooking time. Asparagus requires long cooking time once dried.

BEANS (Kidney, Pinto)

Cook raw according to directions. Drain and place on trays. If using canned kidney beans - drain, rinse and place on trays. Dry 8-12 hours. This is a great use for beans if you need them in a hurry for quick baked beans or hurry-up soups. They store well and cooking time will be cut down. To reconstitute beans just add water to cover let set 10-20 minutes. Add to casseroles and bean dishes. For soup, just add without reconstituting. Ready in 10-15 minutes.

THERMOS SOUP *(1 serving)*

Fill thermos 3\4 full of hot water (small 8 ounce thermos)

Add rest of ingredients and close thermos.

1 tablespoon low sodium beef bouillon 1\3 tablespoon dried onions

2 tablespoons tomato powder or 1 \4 cup fresh 1 tablespoon dried celery or 1 \4 of fresh carrot 2 tablespoons dried carrots

2 tablespoons dried cooked beans
2 tablespoons other vegetables (mushrooms etc.) 2 teaspoons thyme (optional)

Open in 30 minutes or up to 2 hours. A low fat soup, great to have in car for winter survival!

Total recipe =	129 calories
Approximate	3.5 g fat
Value	35.8 mgs sodium
	0 mgs cholesterol

REFRIED BEANS
(without the fat or lard like store bought! - makes 2 cups)

Excellent potassium source and fiber

1-1\2 cup rehydrated beans
1 tablespoon dried onion powder
1\2 teaspoon garlic powder
dash black pepper
1\2 fresh tomato chopped fine
1 tablespoon taco seasoning (hot or mild)
1 \2 cup water
sprinkle of sugar (it makes it taste salty without having to add salt)
Optional - add 1\4 cup nonfat cheddar cheese or sprinkle with
    cheese flavored substitute

Mash beans with fork while adding water. Add rest of ingredients
    and heat. Use in tacos, burritos or on salad.

Total recipe =	144 calories
Based on	0.5 g fat
¾ cup raw	138 mgs sodium
Pinto	0 mgs cholesterol

Name Brand Approximate Value

See bar graph for comparison to commercially prepared beans,
which often contain lard.

BEANS (Green)

Clean and snip beans. Cut ¼ inch pieces and place on tray to dry. No need to blanch! Dry 10-25 hours. Use in soups and casseroles. Reconstitute by covering with water for 1-2 hours in refrigerator. Best in casseroles or soups.

CREAMY BEANS IN LOW FAT SAUCE (Serves 4)

2 tablespoons butter substitute
3 tablespoons flour
1 cup skim milk
2 cups reconstituted dry green beans (or 1 cup raw green beans)
    pepper to taste
Optional to add 2 tablespoons butter substitute or pepper to taste

In 2 quart glass mix all ingredients except beans. Microwave 3-4 minutes, stirring every minute until thick and bubbly. Add beans. Microwave another 5-10 minutes until beans are heated. Serve.

Per serving =	54 calories
Approximate	0.2 g fat
Value	33.3 mgs sodium
	0 mgs cholesterol

BROCCOLI

Clean broccoli, cut off florets and place on tray.
Stem portions should be cut into ¼ pieces.
Dry 12-19 hours until brittle. Can be used in salads, casseroles, or sauces. Reconstitute 1-2 hours in refrigerator.

CABBAGE

1 whole dried cabbage fits into a one quart jar! Shred cabbage and place on tray to dry. Dry 8-12 hours until crisp (may want to use liner because it might fall through trays). Use in soups and casseroles. Reconstitute 15-20 minutes. Not necessary to reconstitute for soups or casseroles.

CABBAGE VEGETABLE SOUP (Serves 6)

1 medium potato, peeled and cut in small pieces 1 \2 cup dried cabbage or 1 cup raw 4 cups hot water
1 cans (16 oz) whole tomatoes
1 package frozen vegetables (or 1 cup dried)
1 tablespoon low-sodium beef bouillon granules 1 tablespoon dried
    onion
1 teaspoon dried parsley flakes
1 tablespoon Worcestershire sauce
Put in 3 quart casserole dish combine potato, cabbage and water. Microwave for 5-10 minutes on high. Add remaining ingredients and microwave 17-25 minutes until potatoes are soft.

Per serving =	132 calories
Approximate	3.3 g fat
Value	201.3 mgs sodium
	0 mgs cholesterol

CARROTS

Wash, and peel carrots. Slice 1 \4 inch thick. Dry 12-18 hours. Dried carrots will be hard and brittle. Use in casseroles and soups. I usually combine mine with broccoli in a quart jar, because the colors look good together. Reconstitute 15-30 minutes in water.

CARROT RAISIN SALAD (Serves four ¼ cup servings)
½ cup dried shredded carrots (reconstituted) or 1 cup fresh
shredded carrots
1 cup raisins
2 tablespoons plain nonfat yogurt
Pinch of sugar

Mix together and chill 1 hour before serving.

Per serving =	125 calories
Approximate	0.2 g fat
Value	19.4 mgs sodium
	0.1 mgs cholesterol

CELERY

Clean and chop celery into 1\4 inch thick slices. Dry 8-16 hours.

Dried celery will be crisp. Use in casseroles and soups. Reconstitute 15-30 minutes in water to cover celery. May use as in soups.

CORN

Clean and husk corn. Use knife to take kernels off corn cob (I use my electric knife). Place on plastic wrap lined tray as kernels will fall through tray if not lined. Dry 12-18 hours. Use in chowders, soups, and casseroles. This is the way the Indians stored corn; no need for blanching. Rehydrate 30-60 minutes covered in enough water. Corn will still be a little wrinkled looking. Cornmeal is made by grinding corn up in blender. I usually add a dash of paprika.

FALL CORN CASSEROLE (Serves 8)

Reconstitute 2 cups of corn to equal 2 cups of corn (approximately 1
  cup dried) 1 can cream style corn
3 egg whites
1 cup skim milk
1-8.5 oz box corn muffin mix OR 1 \2 cup flour, 1 tablespoon sugar,
  1 \3 cup cornmeal, and 1 teaspoon low sodium baking powder.

Mix ingredients together. Bake at 350 for 45 minutes. May add
reconstituted pepper for added flavor.

1 serving with corn mix =   219 calories
Approximate Value   4.2 g fat
                        410.9 mgs sodium
                        15.9 mgs cholesterol

1 serving with flour, sugar, etc. = 149 calories

                        1.0   g fat
                        212.3 mgs sodium

                        0.5 mgs cholesterol

CUCUMBERS

Wash and peel cucumber. Slice 1 \4 thick. Dry 6-18 hours until crisp
and they snap when broken. Dip in barbecue sauce or sprinkle with
taco seasoning before drying for different flavor. Eat as snack item
or with dip. Dried cucumbers can be added to any homemade
dressing once reconstituted to add extra flavor. Reconstitute 15-20
minutes in water to cover cucumber slices. Cucumbers will not
reconstitute to full size.

EGGPLANT

Wash and cut into 1 \4 inch thick pieces. May dip in barbecue sauce or taco sauce before drying. Dry 12-19 hours. Reconstitute in water to cover 1-2 hours in refrigerator. Use in casseroles or soups.

Kale- dry leaves on tray 10-25 hours. Kale will easily flake and brittle to the touch. Powder in a blender and use in soups. Kale is found to contain nutrients that help fight off breast cancer!

MUSHROOMS

Clean and slice into 1 \4 inch thick slices. An egg slicer works great to slice mushrooms. Dry 12-18 hours. Reconstitute by covering with water for 25 minutes. Use in pizza, casseroles, soups, and spaghetti sauces.

CREAM SOUP - MUSHROOM (Serves 4)

1 cup dried mushroom (2 cups raw) 2 cups water
2 cups nonfat dry milk
1 tablespoon dried onion
1 tablespoon dried parsley
1 tablespoon all-purpose flour
1 /8 teaspoon ground pepper to taste

Combine all ingredients in blender. Mix until thick and foamy. Mixture will still be lumpy. Pour mixture back into saucepan and heat slowly, stirring with a wire whisk to keep from burning. For cream of chicken soup, add low sodium chicken bouillon to mixture. Add powdered vegetables such as broccoli, etc., for cream of broccoli soup, or dried onion for onion soup.

Total recipe =	143 calories
Approximate	0.4 g fat
Value	189.7 mgs sodium
vs.	
Name brand =	314 calories
10.5 oz. can	23 g fat
	2470.5 mgs sodium

See bar graphs for comparison to commercially purchased
   mushroom soup.

ONIONS

Clean, peel, and chop like you would for onion rings. Dry 12-18 hours. Onions that are dried should crack like a soup cracker. If the onions are brown, the temperature is to hot or you need to rotate your trays more frequently. No need to rehydrate, use as is. For fancy fried onions that are less expensive than the canned fried onions, coat onion with deep fry coating. Deep fat fry then dehydrate. Only store 2 months, preferably in freezer. Add to casseroles, stir fry, and soups as is. If house guests do not leave, dry some onions, and I'm sure you'll be alone!

PEAS

Clean, and place on tray. Dry 25-30 hours until hard and not moist to touch. Use in soups, stews, and casseroles. Reconstitute by covering with water and soaking 25 minutes. The peas can fall through tray if pea size is small, so line tray if necessary.

SPLIT PEA SOUP (Serves 4)

4 cups hot water
½ cup dried peas
1 medium peeled, potato
1 medium carrot, peeled and cubed

2 small slices Canadian bacon

2 tablespoons dried onion flakes

1/3 teaspoon dried parsley

1/3 teaspoon dried oregano

1/8 teaspoon pepper

1/8 teaspoon of minced garlic

Combine ingredients in large casserole.
Microwave 40-50 minutes, stirring every 10 minutes.

1 serving = 147 calories
Approximate   1.3 g fat
Value   198.4 mgs sodium
6.7 mgs cholesterol

PEPPERS (Red, orange, yellow or green)

Wash peppers. Cut into 1 \4 inch thick or thinner slices. Dry 16-24 hours until brittle and feel like dried cut grass. Red peppers mixed with the other peppers are very appetizing. The mixture, once reconstituted, can be used in casseroles, soups or garnish to dress up winter blahs. Use reconstituted peppers on top of pizza. Rehydrated 20 minutes by covering with water. Use to top pizza.

POTATOES (White)

Sliced Potatoes

5 lbs potatoes, scrubbed clean (peeled, if desired)

Dehydrated Sliced Potatoes (Dried) Recipes

Put a large pot (12 quart?) of water on to boil. A water bath canner works well, or you could do smaller batches in a smaller pot. In my book, it's quicker and much easier to use a large pot.
Have a sink full of cold water ready.
Slice potatoes using either a corkscrew slice or a mandolin.
Rinse potatoes with cold water, making sure all slices are separated from each other.

Gently put the potatoes in boiling water (don't get burnt!) and stir well to make sure potatoes are separated.
Let cook 3 minutes. Drain potatoes and plunge them into the cold water to stop the cooking; stir to make sure they are cooled.
They should be dry to the point of snapping when done.
Store in a cool, dry place in a covered glass jar. Or thick closed plastic bag. ** Best if you use freshly dug potatoes.

POTATOES (Sweet and pumpkin)

Clean potatoes or pumpkin. Cut off ends or take top off of pumpkin. Pierce with knife. Cook in microwave until soft - 10-20 minutes on high. Once cool, take skin off and place sections of sliced potato or pumpkin in dryer. Dry until crisp. Rehydrated 35 minutes in water. Use in recipes such as cookies, breads, pie, etc.

PUMPKIN PANCAKES (Serves 14)

2 egg whites
1 1/4 cups skim milk
1 /4 cup powdered dry pumpkin or ½ cup fresh in cubes
¾ cup white flour
¾ cup whole wheat flour
2 teaspoons baking powder (low sodium) 2 tablespoons sugar 1 /2
teaspoon cinnamon ¼ teaspoon nutmeg 2 tablespoons vegetable
oil

Combine all ingredients - stir well. Pour on hot griddle that has been
lightly oiled. Flip pancakes over when bubbles break.

Per serving =	84 calories
Approximate	2.2 g fat
Value	18.9 mgs sodium
	0.4 mgs cholesterol

TOMATOES

Wash and remove the stem. Slice end of the tomato off. Gently
squeeze juice from tomato into saucer. Use this liquid for soups,
casseroles etc. Cut squeezed tomato into slices 1 \4 inch thick. Dry
24-30 minutes until crisp. Rehydrated by covering with water for 25
minutes. Tomatoes that are dried can be powdered to use for
sauces, soups, and casseroles. Even if I use canned tomato sauce, I
will drop dried tomatoes in the sauce for added flavor and an
appetizing look. For cherry tomatoes slice in half and dry until they
feel like a raisin. Remove from dryer and enjoy eating. Very sweet! I
like the pear tomatoes for this too. Store in refrigerator as they can
spoil as they are not fully dry!

Tomato leather can be made by pureeing tomato and pouring on
plastic lined trays ¼ inch thick. Once dry, pulverize and use to make
tomato sauce, etc., or add to soups.

TOMATO SAUCE (thick style - makes 2 cups)

Place 1 cup dried tomato slices (or 2 cups raw) in blender and add
1 1\4 cup water.
1\2 teaspoon powdered onion
1 clove garlic
1\4 teaspoon black pepper
1 \4 teaspoon oregano
1 \4 teaspoon basil
sprinkle of sugar (makes it taste salty)

Blend ingredients well - makes 2 cups.

Total recipe =	81 calories
(2 cups)	0.9 g fat
Approximate	29.9 mgs sodium
Value	0 mgs cholesterol

vs.

Name brand =	147 calories
(2 cups)	0.8 g fat
	2964.5 mgs sodium
	0 mgs cholesterol

Tomato sauce may be prepared and dried in the form of leather and stored. To reconstitute add enough water to cover. Simmer until dissolved.

Great for camping or hiking!
See bar graph for comparison to commercially purchased tomato sauce.

Dried Tomato Basil Pesto

¼ cup dried tomatoes, crumbled
2-3 cloves minced garlic
1 tbsp. extra virgin olive oil
1 tbsp. dried basil
½ cup water

Sauté garlic in olive oil -- do not brown! Turn down heat, add dried tomatoes and basil, stir to coat. Immediately add water and stir. Cover and steam 2-3 minutes until tomatoes are plumped. Serve with pasta. Keeps well in refrigerator. (Note: Omit basil for Dried Tomato Pesto.)

BBQ SAUCE

1 tablespoon powdered onion
1 teaspoon powdered garlic
1\2 cup dried tomato slices or 2 cups fresh ripe tomatoes
2 cups water
1 tablespoon brown sugar or white
1 tablespoon Worcestershire sauce
2 teaspoons prepared mustard
I\ 4 cup vinegar

Blend together well. Pour over chicken. Makes about 1 3\4 cup.

Total recipe =	175 calories
(2 cups)	1.3 g fat
Approximate	367 mgs sodium
Value	0 mgs cholesterol
vs.	
Name brand =	375 calories
(2 cups)	9 g fat
	4075 mgs sodium
	0 mgs cholesterol

Also can be a great marinade for jerky. See bar graph.

SPAGHETTI SAUCE (Makes 2 cups)

2 tablespoon onion flakes
1 1\2 tablespoons sugar
1 teaspoon dried basil
1 teaspoon dried oregano
1 \2 teaspoon garlic powder
1\4 teaspoon marjoram
1 can tomato paste or equivalent of 2\3 cup tomato sauce from
    above or 2 cups raw tomatoes

Blend ingredients and simmer. Serve over spaghetti.

Total recipe = version)	187 calories	(Based on raw tomato
Approximate Value	1.0 g fat 32 mgs sodium 0 mgs cholesterol	
vs.		
Name brand = (2 cups)	515 calories 20.5 g fat 2440 mgs sodium 45 mgs cholesterol	

The spaghetti sauce can be made (I prefer fresh tomatoes and poured on a plastic wrap lined tray then dried as a leather. Once the sauce is dry it should be shiny and not sticky. This can be taken along on camping trips - just add water to cover and simmer until dissolved. Instant spaghetti sauce!

See bar graph for comparison to commercially purchased spaghetti with meatball sauce.

ZUCCHINI

Use smaller zucchini with skin on or if larger, skin and take out seeds. Cut slices 1 \4 inch thick. Dry 8-16 hours until brittle.

Variations:

Dip in BBQ sauce or taco sauce before drying for a different flavor.

Reconstitute by soaking in water 20-30 minutes. For bars, cakes, etc., add extra 1\4 cup water to the batter with reconstituted zucchini.

BEEF AND POULTRY

Optimum temperature for drying jerky is 1400 to 145°.

Meat should be cooked before using in jerky. I usually make a roast and use the leftovers. The meat needs to have reached an internal temperature of 160°. This kills the bacteria that can cause food poisoning, such as E Coli. I use the leftovers and soak in marinade, then dry. Use only lean meats as fat turns rancid very fast. Soak in marinade 1-2 hours or overnight. Marinades are high in sodium. It is difficult to know amount of marinade absorbed to calculate calories, sodium, and cholesterol. Amounts are not listed for marinade.

Great for using Thanksgiving turkey leftovers. Soak leftover turkey in marinade. Dry 12 to 14 hours. Leftover turkey only stores 3 days so use leftovers right after Thanksgiving.

BEEF, TURKEY, OR DEER JERKY

Bake roast, ground chuck, or ground round. Remove fat and bone. Mix marinade together and soak in mixture, stirring so marinade touches all meat. Marinade for 1 \2 day to overnight.

1-2 pounds cooked meat - make sure meat is thoroughly cooked, this will destroy bacteria

Marinade
1 \4 teaspoon each of ginger, powered onion, dried powered garlic
   and ground pepper dash of nutmeg
2 tablespoons of Worcestershire sauce
1 \2 cup light soy sauce
splash of liquid smoke or 1\2 cup of prepared coffee
pinch of brown sugar
Remove meat from marinade. Cut into 1 \4 inch strips (across the grain works best). Dry meat on trays until it cracks apart when put under pressure with fingers.

May use barbecue sauce or taco seasonings for marinade. Other wild game, such as pheasant, can be used as jerky also.

YOGURT

1 tablespoon yogurt with active cultures 1 cup skim milk warmed to 100° 1 tablespoon powered milk

Mix together, pour in microwaveable glass containers (make sure they fit in your dryer). Cover with plastic wrap and dehydrate at 110° for 8-12 hours. Yogurt should be firm when gently shaken. Can be used for sour cream. Also to flavor for snack, place 1 heaping tablespoon of dry Jell-O and add favorite fruit.

Total recipe =	120 calories
Approximate	0.5 g fat
Value	177.2 mgs sodium
	6.1 mgs cholesterol

Yogurt may be substituted for sour cream or mayonnaise in recipes. If heating the yogurt in a prepared casserole, add 2 teaspoons cornstarch before adding to make the yogurt stay thick.

BRUNCH FRUIT DIP (16 tablespoons)

8 ounces nonfat yogurt
2 tablespoons orange, peach or strawberry marmalade.
Mix together and serve with sliced fruit for a sweet dip.

Per tablespoon:	15 calories
Approximate	0 g fat
Value	11.3 mgs sodium
	0.2 mgs cholesterol

YOGURT CHEESE

1 8 oz. plain nonfat yogurt (or 1 cup homemade)

Place yogurt in cheesecloth. Let drain in strainer with dish below to catch moisture (in refrigerator).

Add dried herbs and spice for dip. 1 tablespoon onion powder
3 tablespoons parsley
4 teaspoons dill weed
1 teaspoon sugar (to make yogurt taste salty)

Total recipe =	0.4 g fat
Plain Yogurt	173.6 mgs sodium
Cheese	4.0 mgs cholesterol
Approximate	
Value	
(without herbs)	

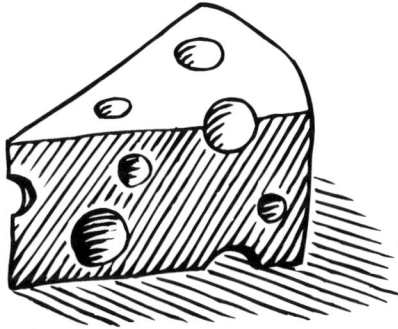

LOW FAT STROGANOFF (Serves 4)

¾ lb ground round steak or sirloin
¼ cup dried mushroom or 1 /2 cup fresh 2 tablespoons dried onion flakes 2 teaspoons low sodium beef bouillon ½ cup water
2 tablespoons flour
1 cup nonfat plain yogurt (made from skim milk) 1/8 teaspoon black pepper (optional)

Brown and drain meat. Add rest of ingredients. Cover and cook until meat is done and sauce is thick (about 45 minutes). Serve over noodles or rice.

Per serving =	215.1 calories
Approximate	7.0 g fat
Value	128.3 mgs sodium
	52.2 mgs cholesterol

HOT FUDGE SAUCE (Makes 1 cup, 16 tablespoons)

3 tablespoons dry cocoa
1\3 cup sugar*****   can use Splenda sweetener instead
1\3 cup skim milk
1-8 ounce nonfat plain yogurt
2 tablespoons cornstarch
1 teaspoon vanilla

Combine ingredients, except vanilla, in 2 quart saucepan. Slowly heat mixture. Stirring often. Gently boil and remove from heat when thickened. Add vanilla and serve, or refrigerate for later use.

Per tablespoon =	33 calories
Approximate	0.2 g fat
Value	13.7 mgs sodium
	0.4 mgs cholesterol

	Vs.	
Name brand	=	62 calories
		2.5 g fat
		21.5 mgs sodium
		2.2 mgs cholesterol

May also add a splash of liquid peppermint flavoring for added flavor.
See bar graph for comparison to commercially prepared hot fudge.

CHILI MIX

3C. dried beans (pink, red, kidney, or sorted)
Seasoning packet:
3 T. chili powder
2 T. dried Minced onion
1 T. dried minced garlic
1 tsp. dried oregano
2 tsp. sea salt
½ tsp. cayenne pepper (opt.)

Can place in covered glass jars and ready to go!

Chili:
1 (8 oz.) can tomato sauce
2 (14 oz.) cans diced tomatoes or ½ cup dried tomatoes and add 1 cup water extra
1 lb. ground beef
10 C. Water

Remove seasoning packet from chili mix and set aside. Rinse beans and place in a large soup pot. Add water and seasoning chili mix. Cook for about 1 to 1 ½ hour. Meanwhile, brown ground beef and drain off fat. Add meat, tomatoes and sauce to the beans. Simmer to blend flavors for approximately 20-30 minutes.

SANDWICH SPREAD (16-18 tablespoons)

8 ounces plain yogurt.
2 tablespoons gourmet-style mustard

Mix together, and serve with low fat crackers, or vegetables. Use sandwich spread as nonfat alternative to mayonnaise.

Per tablespoon =   8 calories
Approximate   0 g fat
Value   30.5 mgs sodium
                       0.2 mgs cholesterol

LOWFAT DRESSING

1 \2 cup plain low fat or nonfat plain yogurt (if you use skim milk)

1 \4 c seasoned gourmet rice vinegar (at health food stores) or use vinegar that you have placed favorite herbs in for a couple of days

1 tablespoon dried onions

Pinch of sugar (this makes it taste salty without adding salt)

Mix well. Excellent on cucumbers.

Total recipe =   88 calories
Approximate   2 g fat
Value   88.1 sodium
                       2.0 mgs cholesterol

APPLE CINNAMON PANCAKE MIX

3 cups all-purpose flour
4 tsp. cinnamon
2 ¼ T. sugar
2 T. baking powder
1 ¼ tsp. salt
¾ C. dried apple pieces
(can mix and store in baggies or in glass jars until needed for all ingredients above)
To make 5 servings:
1 1/3 C. Apple Cinnamon Pancake mix shown above.
¾ C. milk
1 egg
2 T. vegetable oil

In medium bowl, combine milk, egg and vegetable oil. Mix in the mix until moistened but still has lumps. Heat a lightly oiled griddle or frying pan over medium/high heat. Pour batter, ¼ C. at a time on to prepared girdle. Cook on both sides until golden/brown. Flipping when surface begins to bubble

JAMBALAYA MIX

3 C. long-grain white rice
2 ½ T. dried minced onion
2 ½ T. green bell pepper flakes
2 bay leaves (opt.)
2 T. plus 1 tsp. beef bouillon granules
1 ¼ tsp. garlic powder
1 ¼ tsp. pepper
1 ¼ tsp. dried thyme crushed red pepper
7 ½ C. water
1 (20 oz,) can tomato sauce
1 ¼ C. cooked hams or smoked sausage
1 ¼ C. cooked shrimp

Combine all except the ham or sausage and shrimp, in to a large skillet. Reduce heat to simmer; add ham or sausage and cook for 20 min. Add shrimp and cook another 5 min. put bay leaves on top of dish ONLY for looks.

CHILI TOMATOE MAC MIX

½ C. plus 2 T. instant dry milk
1/3 C. cornstarch
1 T. plus 1 tsp. chicken or beef bouillon granules
2 tsp. dried minced onion
¼ tsp. plus 1/8 tsp dried basil
¼ tsp. plus 1/8 tsp dried thyme
¼ tsp. plus 1/8 tsp pepper
2 tsp. dried parsley flakes
1 tsp. garlic powder
2 T. chili powder
3 C. macaroni
(May mix and save in container at this point)
1 ½ lbs. ground beef
3 (15 oz.) cans chopped tomatoes
2 C. water

In a large skillet, brown ground beef and drain off fat. Add all ingredients above with ground beef in skillet. Simmer covered 20 min or until macaroni is tender, stirring often.

VEGITARIAN BLACK BEAN MIX

2 ½ C. dried black beans
  -seasoning portion
3 T. dried minced onion
3 T. dried minced garlic
1 tsp. dried orengo
2 tsp. salt
¼ to ½ tsp. cayenne pepper
1 ½ C. white rice
1 T. olive oil
1 tsp. Salt

Mix all in a large soup pot and simmer for 2 hours. Then steam for 20 min.

GROUND BEEF STROGANOFF

½ C. plus 2 T. instant dry milk
1/3 C. cornstarch
1 T. plus 1 tsp. chicken or beef bullion granules
2 tsp. dried minced onion
3/8 tsp dried basil
3/8 tsp dried thyme
3/8 tsp. pepper
2 tsp. dried parsley flakes
1 tsp. garlic powder
2 C. egg noodles
(can store all of above in glass jar)
1 ½ lbs ground beef
4 C. water
1C. sour cream
in a large skillet brown and wear off the ground beef. add the 4 cups of water and the storable stuff to the skillet and stir. Bring mixture to a boil, reduce heat, cover and simmer for 15 to 20min or until noodles are tender. Top with sour cream and serve immediately.

CHIKEN RICE SOUP
3 C. long grain brown rice
¾ C. chicken bouillon granules
2 T. dried tarragon
2 T. dried parley flakes
½ tsp. pepper
18 C. water
1 ½ T. butter or margarine
1can chicken or 1 C. cubed chicken (opt.)
in large soup pot put in all but the chicken to boil reduce heat and add the chicken if desired. Simmer for 30 to 35 min or until rice is tender

HERBS AND SPICES
1 tablespoon of fresh herb = 1 teaspoon dried herb
1\3 teaspoon powdered herb

ONION POWDER OR GARLIC POWDER

Grind up dried onion or garlic. Keep in jar covered.

Herbs are so easy to grow, and many come back year after year and require little space. Drying the herbs and spices is very easy. Wash leaves, blot dry, remove stem, and dry for 1-5 hours. Dried herbs and spices can make lovely gifts if you place the dry herb or spice in a baby food jar and decorate the cover. It's a gift that's much appreciated.

Whole or dried herbs can be placed in vinegar for a new taste. Let the herbs remain in vinegar, place in warm area, ready to use in 30 days.

ITALIAN SEASONING (Low sodium)

1\4 teaspoon fennel
3 1 \2 tablespoons dried parsley
1 1\2 teaspoon powdered oregano

3 1\2 teaspoons powdered onion

2 teaspoons dried basil

1 1\2 teaspoons ground marjoram

1 teaspoon garlic powder

1\4 teaspoon pepper

Mix together and use 1 \2 of it for 1 quart of sauce. Add 1 tablespoon of sugar and simmer the sauce gently.

POULTRY SEASONINGS (Low sodium)

1 teaspoon dried lemon peel 1 1\2 teaspoons powdered thyme 1
    tablespoon savory
1 tablespoon marjoram
2 tablespoons parsley
1 bay leaf

Mix and place on baked or stewed chicken.

LEMON-PARSLEY FOR FISH (Low sodium)

2 tablespoons lemon juice
1 tablespoon dried parsley
1 teaspoon lemon zest
1/8 teaspoon paprika

Sprinkle over fish. Bake or broil.

CHILI POWDER (Low sodium)

3 tablespoon paprika 2 teaspoons crushed oregano 1 teaspoon
    cumin
1 teaspoon turmeric
1 teaspoon garlic powder
¼ teaspoon cayenne pepper

ROLL & BAKE FOR CHICKEN

1 cup fine whole wheat bread crumbs 1 teaspoon poultry seasoning
    1 /4 teaspoon onion powder 1 /4 c whole wheat flour
1 tablespoon paprika
½ teaspoon pepper
1 teaspoon garlic powder 1 teaspoon marjoram

Mix together. Dip chicken in skim milk. Roll in mixture. Bake at 300°
for 1 hour.

TACO SEASONING (Low sodium)

2 teaspoons chili powder 1 teaspoon paprika
1 teaspoon cumin
1 teaspoon onion powder ¾ teaspoon garlic powder dash of cayenne
  pepper

Use instead of 1 package of taco seasoning.

CROUTONS

Commercially made croutons may contain lard. To make low fat
croutons, slice bread into cubes. Season with butter substitute or
herb mixtures. Dry 1-3 hours. Day-old bread works well as
inexpensive way to make croutons or stuffing.

SEASONED CROUTONS

½ teaspoon onion powder

1 /4 teaspoon garlic powder

¼ teaspoon dill weed

1/8 teaspoon pepper

Add seasoning to bread by gently pressing into 4 slices of bread.
Cube and dehydrate.

Special Occasions

Pansy flower blossoms (make sure not sprayed with harmful herbicides, and insecticides!). Pick after the dew. Place whole flower on dehydrator tray. Dry at 110 temperature 1-2 hours) Flower should be dry and crisp to the touchy like saltine cracker. Place on cake for elegant look! Pansies are edible too for salads!

Hamburger Beef Jerky

5 lbs 90% lean ground beef (90-92%)
4 1/2 teaspoons sea salt
3/4 teaspoon garlic powder
1/2 teaspoon crushed red pepper flakes
2 1/4 tablespoons meat tenderizer
3/4 tablespoon pepper
3 tablespoons brown sugar
1/2 cup Worcestershire sauce
1/2 cup liquid smoke
1/3 cup ketchup

Brown hamburger and cook thoroughly.
Mix all spices with ground beef EXCEPT Worcestershire, liquid smoke and ketchup.
You need to really get your hands in to mix it well.
Press into strips with a jerky gun.
Mix Worcestershire, liquid smoke and ketchup in a shallow dish.
Coat strips with sauce.
Place on trays to dry.
Other flavors as follows:
Hot and spicy - mix Louisiana hot sauce with water to thin a bit. Coat strips and dry.
BBQ - thin your favorite bottled BBQ sauce with water. Coat strips and dry.
Teriyaki - thin bottled teriyaki sauce with soy sauce. Coat strips and dry.

Dehydrator Taco Chips

6 servings   ½ day 10 min prep
Change to: servings US Metric
1 cup whole kernel corn or creamed corn
1 cup sharp cheddar cheese, grated
1/2 cup red peppers or green peppers, diced
1 tablespoon onions, chopped
1/8 teaspoon cayenne pepper
1/2 teaspoon chili powder salt

In a blender or food processor, blend together all ingredients at high speed.
Spread mixture thinly onto Fruit Roll Sheets.
Dry at 130° for approximately 10 hours or until dry on one side.
Lift entire corn ring off of Fruit Roll Sheet, turn over and dry for two hours longer or until crisp.
Break into pieces.

Dehydrator Granny Smith Granola

6 servings   3¼ hours 15 min prep
Change to: servings US Metric
3 granny smith apples
2 cups quick-cooking oatmeal
1/2 cup slivered almonds
2 tablespoons brown sugar
1 tablespoon honey, in
1/4 cup water
1 teaspoon salt
1/2 teaspoon cinnamon

Place in a bowl with the other ingredients and toss lightly until thoroughly mixed.
Place mixture on a Fruit Roll sheet and dry for 2 to 3 hours, or until crunchy.
For a tenderer granola, add 1/4 cup vegetable oil before drying.
Store in an air-tight container.

Fruit Powder

Add a burst of flavor to your favorite recipes, (muffins, cakes, donuts, etc) by adding fruit powder.

How do you make fruit powder?

Dry your fruits so they are extra crispy then place them in a blender on high until powdered. To use this powder in recipes, combine 1/2 c fruit powder to 1 c. of flour. Follow the recipe as directed. This not only adds nutrition, but huge amounts of flavor as well!

In a blender, combine 1/2 c. fruit powder to water or milk, add a couple ice cubes and enjoy a delicious fruit smoothie or milk shake.

Other ideas:

Add 1 T to yogurt for flavored yogurt
Add 1 T. Fruit Powder (any kind of fruit) to homemade oatmeal packets & 1 T. of powdered coffee creamer for Fruit-n-cream oatmeal that your kids will beg for
Add flavor to your waffles & pancakes, sprinkle over your cereal in the morning.

Sun-Dried Tomato Dip

1/4 Cup sun-dried tomatoes
Balsamic vinegar
1/3 Cup sour cream
1/3 Cup mayonnaise
1/3 Cup plain yogurt
2 cloves garlic, finely minced
1 Tbsp fresh basil, chopped (or 1 tsp. dried)
1/4 Cup green olives, chopped

Place tomatoes in a small bowl and add balsamic vinegar until just covered. Allow to soak for about an hour. Remove tomatoes from vinegar and drain well. Chop finely and mix with other ingredients. Keep in refrigerator until ready to serve. Makes 16 Servings

Drying Chile Peppers

**use plastic gloves to clean and slice as they will become very hot on your skin and areas that you touch such as your eyes!

Chile peppers should be harvested for maximum color, when the pods have partially dried on the plant, as the succulent red pods have not fully developed their color. Pod moisture content from red Chile peppers is between 65% and 80%, depending on whether they are partially dried on the plant or harvested while still fresh .

When drying Chili peppers, select the freshest pod. Wash and remove any damaged areas that have cuts, breaks or spoil spots. Cut into even pieces.

For green chili peppers: Wash. To loosen skins, cut slit in skin, then rotate over flame 6-8 min. or scald in boiling water. Peel and split pods. Remove seeds and stem.

Dehydrator Delights Reorder

Dehydrator Delights
By Noreen Thomas
12506 20th St N
Moorhead, MN 56560

Please send_____copies of your cookbook at $7.97 per copy. I have included $3.50 per copy for shipping and handling. Enclosed is my check or money order.

Your Name:

_____

Your Address:

_____

Your City, State, Zip:

_____

Book Cost _____ Books x $7.97 = $_____

Handling & Shipping _____ Books x $3.50= $_____

Tax if applicable $_____

Send check or money order for $_____

Website: www.hcity.com

966473

Made in the USA